It Is What It Is

Dalton Hoferer

BookLeaf Publishing

India | USA | UK

Presentation by *BookLeaf Publishing*

Web: www.bookleafpub.com

E-mail: info@bookleafpub.com

ISBN : 9789357449038

First edition 2021

DEDICATION

Dedicated to the one who opened this world of writing up to me. Allowing me to share myself in their world and accepting me for who I am. To Sunshine.

I'll give you my all,

To the point of exhaustion

And still keep giving.

ACKNOWLEDGEMENT

Special thanks to the publisher for providing this unique opportunity to someone so undeserving. Thank you to everyone who has supported me throughout my life to include the people who said I wouldn't amount to anything!

PREFACE

This is just a collection of poems that I have written to better understand some of the thoughts that circulate through my head. There isn't a theme or direction, but more of an outlet to let some of my experiences or thoughts to fall out. I have endured many things through out my life and never really had an outlet to express it all. I started to get more involved with my mental health and began exploring different ways to manage it. I eventually met someone who shared their world of poetry writing and performing. It has been quite a unique adventure to start writing and seeing how I am able to put sentences together to form, what I believe, to be something worthwhile.

Noise

I've killed myself, more than once

Not literally, God no

But in my mind, every which way

I have done it

It would happen randomly

Whether alone or with others

I couldn't tell you why

As I truly don't have an answer

Maybe it was an escape

From things that my mind didn't want to bare

Things that have happened, reliving mistakes

Or was it a secret out that was hidden inside

Secretly telling myself there is always an escape

I've killed myself many times

It's problematic I know

It isn't something I wanted

Like a whisper in my ear

A call to the void

But only I could hear it

Trying to push it off like a playful jab

At my inner sanity

The gentle bullying of my inner self

I've tried to kill myself, once

This time the voice got too loud to take

Screaming in the back of my head

Louder than everything else.

But when I was yearning for silence

Noise brought me back, ringing

Slow and stuttered words upon listening ears

Allowing memories to drown the scream

I used to kill myself, only in my mind

But the only thing I killed was the scream inside

Green Eyes

Soft and deliberate
Steps on uneven ground
Natural silence
Hunting what doesn't want found

Set of twelve
Walking toward familiar unknown
Ready for uncertainty
Prepared for yet to be shown

Eyes of green
Cutting through the black
Phantoms of violence
Approach of determined tact

Ghosts pressed against doors
Flowing through as if water
Inspecting every nook and corner
No words, as if mind readers

Unexpected visitors
Disturbing terrors sleep
Tied and blinded
Surgically removed, tidy and neat

Gone as quietly as arrived
Vanishing in mechanical air
No trace of disturbance
None is lost, all is fair.

Giants

Leering in the horizon

Lies dark giants

Staring in my direction

Body of shadows

With eyes of white

The weight of their gaze

Affecting most aspects of life

The vibrations of their steps

Felt in my bones

Of it walking closer

To stare above me

Their presence heavy

Like a dense fog

Judging everything done

Or ever do

Not saying a word

But their gaze is always known

Isn't it Funny?

Isn't it funny?

How naïve uncertainty

Can create false security

Ignorance to what's inflicted

Isn't it funny?

Allowing yourself to cease

For someone else

Who claims love

Isn't it funny?

They keep possession

Of what used to be you

Locked away, denied to access

Isn't it funny?

The one who "loves"

You want to escape

Even at the pain involved

Isn't it funny?

That once you can finally see

 Your reflection of your old self again

Can you actually begin to laugh

One Down, Four Up

One down
Release tension
Feet slide on earth

One up
Twist increase
Leaning into torque

Two up
The thunder increases
Silencing the inward noise

Three up
Wind begins to whip
stripping away the woes

Four Up
Gliding over concrete
into flying bliss

Sleep

Kicks
In the back
Hanging
On the Edge
Freezing
Except for a piece
Hearing
snores of a little one
Never
Slept better

Overly Simple

Placed on the lateral thigh
Lay the Dorsal hand of mine
Phalanges entwined
Together with another
Muscles contracting
To clasp the others tightly
Living sheets of soft silk
Transferring currents
That travel radially
To the rhythmic creation within
Causing a melting rift
Maintaining the intimate grasp
For perceived eternity

I'm Good

How are you?
I'm doing great.

Wait

No that's a lie
I'm average at best
The stress I put on myself
Is starting to wear on me
This existential crisis
Looming over us
Is beginning to grow
Considerably so
And I don't know how to cope
...
So yeah, I'm good

Reflection

I look at my reflection

Staring back into my soul

Studying who I am

A man

Strong enough for everyone

But himself

Not giving time

To self-reflect

Instead selling it

To the people around him

The reflection of the man

Isn't proud

But sees someone trying

Inner Monologue

Where do I belong?

Being interested in everything

Trying to fit in a puzzle

But coming from a different box

Finding Solice in things heavy

But getting lost in the soft beauty's

Of the world around

Never quite fully accepted

Imposter syndrome among friends

Attempting to add vocally

But never heard audibly

Standing in the corner

Of a crowded room

Ready to leave

Leaves

Creating complex veins
strewn across crisp clouded skies
circulating precious life
to what will soon decay

All attempts to hold
through icy breezes
withering slowly
to the shortened sun

Neighbors begin to fall
fluttering gracefully downward
losing sight of the
dulling earth below

Hoping to last
through one more frosted night
until what tethers
releases

House

These memories haunt this house
that is my head.
attempts to exercise them
end with smoke dancing off the tongue
Shifting weights
send creaks rippling
through the foundation
of the soul
Aching reminders
of figures of past times.
Standing in the peripherals
vanishing upon focusing
reappearing somewhere else
Establishing it still there

Crack Open

I don't know
where to even start
should I just talk about my day
or should I water down my past?
Should I keep what keeps me up
to myself or lay it on thick
like wet concrete, swallowing you whole.
What if they ask questions?
Should I indulge or keep it short and sweet?
Will they try to lock me away involuntarily?
Because my mind is a banned snuff film
of trials and tribulations that no one should
witness.
Kept in my private collection with no label,
so only I can pick it out.
Would I be judged for the things
that happen in my life
Whether my choice or not.
What if I don't like their take?
Or they want to try and sedate,
throwing medication in my face?
Which in turn make these expressions
that I am barely strong enough to show fake?
I want to think freely,
like leaf's from trees.

Flowing their own way from the wind.
But I'm worried that I will get raked up
into a bag so black, turned into mulch.
Spread out around thinned,
for easier digestion.
Will they still think I am the same
or will they distance themselves
from who they thought they know,
leaving me to start over.

Poppies

Every step forward
the earth shifts
under the weight I carry
the sun unrelenting
beating upon our backs
At eighteen hours,
only halfway done
traversing in silent columns
over jagged rock
and ancient fields
overlooked by herders
of a different world
a step back in time.
Both wanting peace,
even with different outcomes
their children scamper
with innocent smiles
trading what they have
for delicacies never tasted
a ruffle of hair
time taken to play
we may be quite different
but still sort of the same

Powder

Thousands fall
floating from the sky
None like the one before
unique, yet vulnerable
to a simple touch

Dampening our world
with a symphony of silence
creating a spotless wonder
free of movement
except for the winds cold kiss

Three Cups

I am three cups deep
into this dark muddy water
this warmth filling slowly
the soul within
completing little connections
between the mind
allowing for jittered strength
to take on the day

I am three cups deep
into this amber, cold glass
this burn filling quickly
the void within
separating the connections
from the heart
dulling all memories
holding me to the past.

It's Dark

Giggling in the dark
at the shadows telling jokes
the mechanism of deflection
of ones personal pain
Laughing at the ghosts
the plague the corners of my mind
these monsters that encapsulate
this smile that cannot be
because of the context
it truly isn't funny
the laughter, a side affect
of things wanted hidden
To move past the horrors
I will snicker away

Sunrise War

In the dim morning hours
lays a battle over the horizon
light entangling with dark
Trying to bring a new day
while the dark holding the past
these fleeting seconds flowing
through a colander of flesh
grasping intently to not forget
Holding on to the youth of yesterday
not wanting to accept
the changing of the the time
and the tomorrow to come
the internally screaming
of the battle to stop
just for a moment
to take everything in
making the second last a year
praying to relive what's gone
with nothing but mental photographs
being what holds us there.

Bones

The skeleton inside
sometimes fights interanlly
trying to escape from
the moldy peel that contains
I try to blame these bones
for the uncomfortable feeling
of laying in this skin
But no one blames the bird
from hatching out the egg
So I guess I cannot blame
trying to be free.

Sympathy

There you lie
with a flag draped,
headed to your
final resting place.
The loss of you
reverberates inside.
All these memories
to remind me of the times
but not allowing me to forget
there will be no more.

Sweet Release

Completion of something new
struggling to comprehend the words
that tumble inside this vessel
like a dryer with clothes.
You have done it as well
making it through
this word vomit that
I have tried to make sense of
and all I can say is
Thank you.